MY CLIENT THE FBI

How a Real Estate Appraiser
Assisted the FBI
Before and After
the Mortgage Crisis
In Cleaning Up a Broken System

Donald J. Gossman, SRA

ACKNOWLEDGMENTS

To my children Daniel and Rachel who didn't choose to go through this journey with their dad but were by his side the whole time.

To my dad Ralph and mother Jeanne who taught and showed me right from wrong, and to do right even when it is costly.

To my sister Teri and brothers Mike and Steve for moving ten times with me when we were young, and always being there for me.

To my friends who encouraged me to write my story to share it with the public. (Long live the sand.)

To Fate for allowing me to be in the right place at the right time with the right knowledge and meeting the right people to make a difference in this world.

TABLE OF CONTENTS

INTRODUCTION

L et's make one thing clear: real estate appraisers are not known for a bent toward danger. If you want a high-adrenalin, on-the-edge career, become an astronaut or a drug runner. We appraisers do not have our own action figures; Steven Seagal would never be tagged to play one of us in the movies; pulling out your latest analysis of neighborhood comparables does not work in impressing women.

We get calls from banks and other lending institutions hiring us to determine an accurate value for a property. So we measure, inspect, compare and analyze, and in the end, we provide a fair assessment of what a property is worth.

About as sexy as a CPA or an IRS auditor.

And that was my life for about 28 years, until the day a phone call, then another, changed everything.

The first call came from a mortgage lender, asking me to value a home for twice what I knew it was worth. And the second call was mine, to the FBI, to report a lender dealing in fraud.

Instead of that second call bringing an end to my potential involvement in an illegal and offensive professional breach, it began a relationship with government agents in the middle of work to break a mortgage fraud ring.

That new relationship took me first to the witness stand in a federal courthouse, then into the middle of what would be known as the Mortgage Securities Meltdown of 2008, teaching not just FBI agents, but Department of Justice prosecuting attorneys, mortgage lenders, real estate brokers and others how to recognize – and prevent – mortgage fraud.

An ordinary soccer dad from Leawood, Kansas made a call that he thought would contribute to the integrity of his profession, and wound up on a journey that would take him through cancer and bankruptcy to a role as an anti-fraud spokesman for his profession and beyond.

I'm telling this story for two reasons: first, the Mortgage Meltdown of 2008 cost millions of people their homes and jobs, and our economy came close to collapsing altogether. I don't want that to ever happen again. If telling this story can help you better understand how, as a country, we nearly lost everything, then I want to tell it.

But I have another motivation, too. There are millions of people like me, unrecognizable people working in unimpressive settings who face daily choices about doing the right thing. Fudging, cheating just a little, shading the truth – these come easily when the pressure of those around us and the simple economic realities of our situations push us. We may pay a price for telling the truth, and it is sometimes hard to see that truth telling will make a difference.

I'm here to say it can.

Ordinary people in unremarkable places who speak for what's right, and continue to speak, can make a difference and can influence national scenarios. I know, because I did, and I believe others can, too.

I hope reading my story gives you courage to try.

CHAPTER ONECHAPTER ONE

THE INVITATION

T he phone call wasn't unusual. In 2006 I was a real estate appraiser who'd been doing this work for twenty-eight years and was known for experience with high-end houses. An established business owner with SRA designation since 1991. So a request from a mortgage lender to bring in an appraisal on a higher-end home in a prestigious Kansas City neighborhood was fairly run-of-the-mill.

"The seller and buyer have agreed on a price – about $1.5 million," a mortgage processor identifying herself as Angela from Soldi Financial explained. "We just need a couple of confirmation appraisals to stick in the file and the deal is done."

Angela had just confirmed that the lenders expected my appraisal to come in at over a million, since that loan figure exceeded one million dollars,

4

two, not one, appraisals were required. As we talked I instructed her to fax me the contract and order the appraisal on my website. Good as done.

A signed buyer/seller contract with a purchase price of $1,473,000 showed up within half an hour. I clicked on the MLS website and typed in the address.

What was this?

The MLS showed the house as an active listing for only $699,000 – less than half the price the buyer was agreeing to pay.

Of course buyers sometimes offered above the ask price, but *offering more than double*? And the history of this house showed it had been on the market for more than 18 months with a starting price of $850,000 and had worked its way down over time to $699,000.

Unless the buyer had found an original Van Gogh hidden in the walls or knew the house was built on a Texas-size oil well, no one in her right mind would offer $1.5 million for this house, even in such an upscale area.

I called Angela. "I'm missing something here," I told her. "I'm looking at the MLS listing right now – the house is listed at $699,000 and there are no comparables out there to justify more than that. At the price you're quoting either it's a rehab with some pretty amazing upgrades or I've got the wrong address. Which is it?"

She laughed lightly. "Oh, neither one. You've got the right house, and it hasn't had updates done. But the seller and the buyers have agreed on that $1.5 million, and we need an appraisal from you to come in at that amount."

When the numbers don't add up

I started to feel suspicion. By taking on this job, was I walking into a crooked deal in process?

"Not paranoia on your part," I reassured myself quickly. "You've seen enough of these the past few years to know when somebody ought to be asking questions.

Sometimes a lender would be trying to raise capital by getting more mortgage loans on its books, so it wheedled out ways to inflate values of the homes. Its book of loans got bigger and the value of its business increased. (After all, people *always* pay their mortgages, so if a lender says it loaned $1 million on a home, and sticks that loan into a mortgage securities bundle to sell to another lending institution, who questions it?)

Or a rotten realtor or mortgage broker tried to sneak an unqualified buyer into a house out of their reach. So, the value of the house would be inflated so unsuspecting lenders would pony up for 100% or more of the house purchase price, rather than the 80% or less they thought they were providing.

The easiest way to pull off one of these scams? Get an appraiser in your back pocket. Get him or her to "adjust" the age of the house, or the size, or which neighborhood comparables he chooses - inflate the price - and boom! You've got in hand an "official" report of value that you can literally take to the bank.

All this started in ways that looked fairly innocent. A lender might ask us to consider increasing the value of a home by $2,000 or $5,000 so the borrowers wouldn't have to take out expensive PMI insurance on the loan. If the new value fell within the range of comparables in the current appraiser's report, it was industry practice to agree to the change.

Then we begin to see appraisal orders with the value the lenders required penciled onto the order. "We're just doing a 'value check,'" they'd explain if we asked about it. "We want to see if the property is generally worth what the buyer can afford."

One or two steps away from the line led to larger steps, and before long, too many appraisals simply were lies.

I'd seen hundreds of these rip-off attempts in my twenty-eight years in appraising, and reported a batch of them to regulatory boards; enough that I'd become an appraisal reviewer for one board, tasked with evaluating evidence that might lead to an appraiser losing a license, and a livelihood.

In the past six years, it seemed like the frequency of attempts at appraisal fraud were on the rise, and not just incrementally. (I would later learn that from 2004 to 2009 a full 44% of real estate appraisals were intentionally fraudulent. But at the time of the call, I just knew something was going very wrong in the world of real estate mortgages, and faster all the time.)

And I had gotten tired of it. Tired enough to consider changing my business model away from the 14-employee business I ran to a small specialty appraisal business I could manage from my basement office. A divorce in 2002 left me with full custody of two pre-teen children; this dictated the timing of my decision to cut back the scope of the business. These two kids were going to need more from me than the leftovers of 60- to 70-hour workweeks.

A simpler business, and working from home met two needs: more availability for the kids, and less need to compete for work I wasn't sure was ethical.

Now I was being offered an enticement to backpedal on that commitment to ethics.

I could feel my chest tighten and my voice grow colder as I asked a couple more questions of Angela to test my hunch. Her answers didn't reassure me this deal was on the up-and-up.

Count me out

"I don't do those kinds of appraisals," I told her in a clipped voice.

Would she pick up on my inference that the appraisals I referred to weren't honest? Would she come back with a stuttered cover story to defend her request?

She ignored the implications of what I'd said.

"No problem," she responded quickly. "We have a long list of appraisers who probably will give the valuation we need. I'll just call the next one."

And she hung up.

It was her breezy tone that did it, and the unstated assumption that appraisers operated like pick-a-value vending machines. Insert enough cash, and out will come whatever value you pick on whatever home you choose.

Talk about a woman with bad timing! Angela had started with the wrong appraiser, one who had only the week before learned about a whole new, and far more effective way to help squash mortgage fraud.

Just the week before, I'd attended a fraud seminar offered by the Appraisal Institute of Kansas City. Hearing an ex-con who'd pulled off white collar crimes involving hundreds of millions of dollars (and who had obviously gotten caught) tell us both how he did it, and how common it was shook me to attention.

An FBI agent specializing in investigating mortgage fraud followed him, and she alerted us to fraud rings operating in the city.

I raised my hand in response to so many of the FBI agent's questions about things like silent second mortgages, management fees and inflating sales prices that when I saw her at the break she commented, "Either you know what mortgage fraud looks like or you commit it."

I laughed, and assured her which side of the line was mine. And I got to tell her how encouraging her work was to an appraisal reviewer like me, since I'd been seeing fraud on a near-daily basis for the last six years. We exchanged cards, and decided meeting for lunch some time to compare stories would benefit us both. I drove back to my office feeling better informed and less alone in my disgust at all this. "Maybe the best seminar I've ever been to," I said to myself.

Now, when the moment presented itself, I knew to fish out Agent Jensen's card and make the call. Surely an $800,000 fraud might interest her.

I picked up the phone, and punched in the number of the FBI.

Then, The Call

I'll admit, my voice was pitched a little higher and I talked a little faster than usual when I asked to speak with her, then left a voicemail explaining what had just happened. It wasn't that I thought something would come of this awkward attempt at whistleblowing, or that I'd actually even hear back from her, but the cops-and-robbers kid in me felt a little excitement at being part of a cleanup I'd wanted to see happen for years.

The callback

A call from the FBI came on October 13, 2006 while I was stopped in a drive-through line at the bank, waiting to make a deposit. (Turns out the day was "Friday the 13th." This should have been a hint of what lay ahead, but at that time, everything seemed straightforward enough.)

"It's Agent Jensen," the caller said. "We're interested in the appraisal you were asked to do, and want to know more." I explained where I was and asked to call her back in about 15 minutes when I'd returned to my office and had the paperwork in front of me.

Now at my desk, I was ready for her questions. "Who are the buyers?" she wanted to know.

When I read the names on the contract, she responded evenly, "...part of one of the mortgage fraud rings operating in Kansas City..."

Whoa. This is what she'd talked about at the seminar. So this "fraud ring" stuff wasn't just drama to get our attention. These rings were real and an ordinary guy like me could be invited to join. This was going to make for some pretty attention-getting conversation at soccer games!

"Who are the sellers?" she went on. I read their names, and paused.

Agent Jensen paused too then said briskly, "Let me grab another agent, and we'll be at your office in twenty minutes." No lead-in or explanation; just a heads-up they'd be coming. I was caught off-guard. Do FBI agents usually come to your house to ask their questions? Since the closest I'd ever been to these guys was via television and movies, I had no idea. My appraisal clients didn't even come to my house. What was going on here?

In the midst of straightening up the pile of work-in-progress papers on my conference table, I heard my son Daniel and his friend Joe upstairs.

Oops. I'd forgotten Daniel was home from school today, and Joe was here too. Agent Jensen hadn't said anything about the need to be discreet about our meeting, but what if it mattered? Chatting with Agent Jensen in the middle of a restaurant was one thing; here at my home office was another. I thought I should probably err on the side of caution, and headed upstairs.

I pulled Daniel aside. "We need to take Joe home," I told him.

"Okay," he said. "You mean right after dinner or later?"

"I mean now," I told him.

"Dad! What about the Three-Meal Rule?" he countered. "You know you promised to feed my friends three time in a row before they take a break. Joe's only had two; we owe him."

My boy was right about the rule, but this time, the rule would have to be overridden.

"I'm not going to explain this," I told him, "but I have friends I didn't expect coming over, and Joe can't be here when they arrive."

With a "whatever..." sigh he explained to Joe their time was up, and I loaded both boys in my truck to deliver Daniel's friend. On the way back to our house, Daniel asked with an edge of annoyance, "So, who do you have coming to our house that Joe can't be around?"

Joe was a guest; Daniel lived there. He deserved to know, I thought. "In about fifteen minutes, two FBI agents are going to show up at our house."

This was not the answer he expected, and he turned quickly to me. "Dad, is everything okay?"

It was, of course, or at least I thought so, but I wasn't sure how much to disclose, so I went for simple reassurance. "I haven't done anything wrong," I told him. "Right now we'll leave it at that."

We agreed it was better if Daniel disappeared, so he headed for his room. But I was glad I'd asked him to go when two matching black cars pulled up in front of the house, and the man and woman, both dressed in black suits, and equipped with both badges and guns rang the doorbell. ("Just like the movies," I noted, "but at *my* house?")

Agent Jensen introduced me to Agent Robert Schaefer, a white collar crimes lead investigator. Agent Schaefer was easily 6'4" with a decisive handshake and an impressive bulk of muscle. "I'd assign him to drug busts," I thought to myself. "Seems a little wasted on white collar crime...unless there's something about all this I don't know."

I invited them to my office, and once seated at the conference table they asked me to retell the story of the call, my assessment, and response.

"Are you familiar with the seller's name?" Agent Schaefer wanted to know. I wasn't, so he explained the man's father was a fairly well known Las Vegas mobster in the 1970's who was in the end executed by the mob, his body left stuffed in the trunk of a car.

"But the son, your seller, isn't a part of the mob...as far as we know," Agent Schaefer said evenly, almost off-handedly.

Maybe it was because this whole scene still seemed surreal to me, but having this man with a badge and a gun telling me I was putting myself in opposition to someone who might or might not have mob connections? And he's disclosing this here in my house with my 15-year-old son upstairs? However, I shook off this thought while Agent Schaefer went on.

"Do you recognize the name of the buyer's wife?" I didn't.

"It might help if you heard her public name. It's Katherine Shields."

I straightened. Did I hear correctly? Katherine Shields was the Jackson County Executive who had recently thrown her name into the ring in the race for mayor of Kansas City.

Will you help?

Both agents sat quietly for a moment while I processed what I had just heard. Clearly they'd done this before, and knew enough to move only as fast as I could.

Agent Schaefer spoke again. "These disclosures are going to be helpful," he said, gesturing toward the copy of the contract and work order I'd provided. "So thank you. But we came to ask if you'd be willing to collect some additional information to support the investigation."

"And that would mean...?" I said.

"It would mean calling Angela at Soldi Financial and telling her you'd complete the appraisal."

No guns involved or dead bodies in car trunks.

"I could do that," I said.

"And," Agent Jensen went on, "would you be willing to record the conversation?"

This request didn't seem unreasonable, and with the chance to sleep on it overnight, I figured if I had reservations, there'd be time for them to surface. "I will," I said.

But Agent Jensen was reaching in her briefcase for what turned out to be a recording device, a small silver box with ear buds plugged into the side. When she asked me to record, she meant right here, right now, I realized. My heart started to beat faster but I tried to look cool, like recording conversations for the FBI was as usual for me as Sunday Sand Volleyball.

I said little as she explained how the machine worked, turned it on and noted in a notebook the date, time, location, people present and case name.

So this was how law enforcement gets those recordings they use in court. I put in the ear buds and dialed Angela's number. When she answered, I tried my best to sound all cool and casual. "Angela, Don." Like we're old, best friends.

"About that house and the $1.5 mil appraisal. I was just looking at some comparables in that area, and I think I found some ways I could probably bring it in for about the amount you need."

Previously my "no" had been so firm; now I'm seeking out the work. This had to sound convincing without trying too hard to be believable.

Angela seemed oblivious. "Great," she said cheerfully. "You know we'll need another appraisal too since the loan is over a million. Would you coordinate with the other appraiser we've hired so your two reports come out fairly similar? We want to pass the lender's underwriting guidelines without any problems."

"Just let me know who you're using," I said. "We'll work out any differences before you see the reports."

She thanked me and said she'd call back with the second appraiser's name and contact information. We hung up, and I handed the recording device back to Agent Jensen.

So that was what happened when you did undercover work for the FBI. That wasn't too bad and we caught a crook right in the act.

Next steps

But I realized my self-congratulations and sigh of relief were premature as I saw Agent Jensen reaching in her briefcase for another recording device. "Now, when you talk with Angela, and also the other appraiser, here's another machine you can use," she stated, as if I'd been waiting for this next step.

I flashed back to the fraud conference where we'd met, and the way I'd complained to her about dishonest appraisers and how no one seemed to be doing anything about it. Now I couldn't record just one lousy phone call and back out. I said little as I took the machine, and agreed to let them know as more opportunities to capture important evidence presented themselves. They thanked me, and left.

I tried to appear calm, but I felt a little shaky as I walked them to the door. Doing the right thing was supposed to feel brave and heroic, wasn't it? Then why did I feel like I had just begun to dig myself into a deep hole it might be hard to exit?

CHAPTER TWO

THE STING

I got the chance to use my newly acquired skill in recording phone conversations almost at once.

Twenty-eight years of doing appraisals kicked in. If I moved ahead in what we all knew was standard protocol, everything might seem less suspicious to the "perps" (Not an FBI term, but a shorthand that seemed workable for me right now.) The sheer brazenness of it – so Dick Tracy! – helped me lighten up and feel a little less dread. I'd call the realtor who'd listed the house and arrange a time for the appraisal, then call the other appraiser to ask him to attend so we could do the work together. Nothing unusual about all this.

Okay. Get the two phone numbers in front of me – check. Set up the equipment and plug in the ear buds like I had before – check. Punch in the realtor's number – check. Remember to breathe and keep the words coming slowly – check.

"Michael, this is Don Gossman." Voice casual, confident – like ordering a pizza. Just making a routine appointment, remember?

"I'm appraising your Ward Parkway house for Angela at Soldi, and need to set a time to meet you there so I can do the work."

"Uh, I don't have a key to the house," he said. "I'll have to work on that – maybe we can meet there say, Tuesday?"

The realtor selling a property didn't have access to the house? In twenty-eight years I'd never run across this one, and my mind jumped to possibilities. Was he in on the crime? Was he just allowing his name to be attached to the house so the deal appeared legitimate? Was he somehow getting a kickback from all this? Or was he some clueless dupe, caught up in something bigger than he knew?

"Not your business, Gossman," I told myself. "Just make the appointment." We agreed on a meeting time for the following Tuesday and hung up.

Still recording, I dialed the other appraiser. "Why don't you just send me your drawing of the property, and your appraisal," he responded. "I'll do my part later in the week."

Again, interesting. I knew he probably knew this deal was a set-up, yet had agreed to it. Was he making his work easier by just copying the information I supplied and collecting a check for his report?

Usually, my blood boiled at the idea of other appraisers doing exactly what was happening here, but during our phone call, I could hear a baby crying in the background. He was obviously at home, and had a family. "Sometimes it's not so good guy/bad guy simple," I reminded myself as I turned off the recording device and unplugged my ear buds.

I called Agent Schaefer to report progress; he was pleased. And he asked if I could drop by the FBI office in the Federal Building downtown on Monday to leave the recording device with them, and pick up a new one for the meetings the following week. I said I could.

One of many lessons during this venture into new territory centered on these recording devices. Unlike regular recorders, there was no way I could play back what I had just recorded; nor could anyone without special equipment. So, conversations that could become evidence in a trial were essentially "locked in" and tamper-proof. Interesting.

The weekend

The schedule that weekend looked normal: my daughter's soccer games on Saturday; watching a Kansas City Chiefs game with friends on Sunday afternoon while my kids were with their mom.

But my mind was racing. I knew I hadn't imagined Friday's game-changing events; the FBI recording device was stored safely in my desk at home. What I knew was that I was finally doing on a larger scale what I'd tried before in smaller offenses: trying to bring ethics back into appraising.

But now that the stakes were higher, I didn't know what I was getting into. New questions pressed in.

Before, when I'd reported wrongdoers to licensing boards, or been retained by those boards to investigate questionable behavior, it had actually helped my business. I'd developed a reputation for honest and accurate work so those who needed it – attorneys in legal cases, individuals working to settle with contractors or others who had done poor work, VA loans who had no interest in anything but a reasonable loan on a fairly-valued property – people like these sought me out. The work coming in fit me and my staff of two, and the business was doing well.

Would it work the same if my "whistleblowing" resulted in convictions for high-flyers like a Kansas City mayoral candidate?

And all this business about mob connections of those I would help prosecute? What might that mean – for me, for my kids? Okay…so maybe the stuff I imagined was just television drama, but what if it wasn't?

And in this new space, what might I be opening myself up to from a legal perspective? In twenty-eight years in business I'd seen cases of innocent people sued for the most odd and unreasonable things and lose. What if I'd just created some legal exposure I'd never considered?

At the soccer games, I cheered at all the right times, and even managed some small talk with other parents, but my head was spinning.

By Saturday night, I decided I couldn't resolve most of what alarmed me, but maybe I could get some help on the last question that surfaced, that of legal exposure. I called my friend John, a journalist who'd also been trained as an attorney. He might give perspective from two views – the question of legal unknowns, plus thoughts from his experience reporting on crimes and trials like this one might grow into.

We met Sunday afternoon, and I told the story. John was reassuring. The FBI connection offered protection from legal exposure, he told me. But of course as a journalist he was eager to know more. We agreed on the need to limit disclosure, but I did promise that as soon as the FBI chose to break the story, he'd have an exclusive interview.

Monday morning at the FBI

The FBI office looked imposing – a plain grey-stucco three story building, surrounded by a 10' high iron fence, blast gate, and prominent surveillance cameras. An armed guard met me at the door and walked me past the metal detectors. "Don't I have to go through those?" I asked. "You're an agent, aren't you?" she said, "Agents aren't required to go through screening."

Nice. So now I could pass as an FBI agent. Was that a good or bad thing? "Actually, I'm an appraiser," I told her. But just then Agents Jensen and Schaefer joined us, and we headed for an interrogation room. We talked through the two recorded conversations I was delivering, and I got up to go.

"A few more things," Agent Schaefer said. Apparently you don't just inform for the FBI without completing the paperwork! Another agent came in to take a photo for their files, and delivered the forms to be completed.

Most of the paperwork seemed standard until I came to the place where my signature would relieve the government of responsibility in case of my untimely death. I signed, but not casually! Did these agents have any idea what an ordinary guy like me saw and read in a request like that? I doubted it.

Ah, but the surprise moment – I'd have a code name. Seriously? Who has code names but the president and spies? Again, in a moment of what I was sure was sheer madness, someone suggested "McDreamy."

Did they mean the Patrick Stewart character on *Grey's Anatomy*? Aside from my mom, who had been smitten with my big brown eyes from my birth, I doubted any reasonable observer would have landed on that name for me! But I figured they probably came up with these over-blown names to distract a newcomer like me from the otherwise pretty-grey experience of informing. Ah, but it might impress my kids...that would be worth something. As it turned out, in the weeks ahead I'd have to sign some documents, and even a check as "McDreamy."

"Enjoy it while you can, Gossman," I told myself. "Ain't gonna last."

The appraisal

Tuesday morning Agent Shaffer had arranged to meet me in the parking lot of a grocery store near the house so he could hand off the recording device I'd be using. When he drove up I left my truck and eased into his car.

"Are you ready to go?" he asked.

"Yeah," I managed.

He produced a slightly weathered looking leather portfolio. "This has everything you need to audio and video tape what happens." And then he showed me how to hold it.

I was still processing the portfolio. Somehow from the movies I thought "wearing a wire" meant actually having some device taped to my chest. Of course if this had been the process we never would have met in a grocery store parking lot, but I didn't have a lot to go on about how these undercover things all worked. I had to go over his instructions again, "just to be sure," I told him. But in reality my brain was so abuzz with what was about to happen I only half heard him the first time. We finished the instructions, he turned on the machine, and I headed out for the house.

Heading down Ward Parkway I started singing to the song on the radio until I remembered I was being recorded. "I don't sound bad in the shower," I told myself, "but this voice may not be meant for public consumption."

When I got to the house, I saw a silver Mercedes in the driveway and guessed rightly the realtor would be waiting outside the house. I snapped a photo of the car in the driveway; later I'd be sure I got one of him standing in front of the house. No way later to say he wasn't there.

He was definitely chatty as I started my work. He'd immigrated to the US from Iran after the Shah's fall in 1979, and had been working with investment groups since. He led an investment group intending to buy between 40 and 50 houses in the Kansas City area, he told me, all worth $1 to $2 million.

"And we're doing the same thing in ten different cities," he said. "The money's coming from overseas; we're going to buy these properties and rent them to executives."

Was he just bragging, or was he feeling me out as an accomplice for other transactions like this one? I didn't know, but I did know it was all on tape. The FBI would figure it out; I was glad I didn't have to.

My appraiser-at-work cover must have been convincing because his tone was definitely collegial. "Do you think you'll be able to bring this house in at the value we need?" he asked. I hedged a little, just to be sure he knew the result would look official. "I'll need to run some comparables," I told him, "but at this point, I think it's doable."

When we finished I headed back to meet Agent Schaefer and turn in the recording equipment. I tried to act cool, but my encounter with the real estate agent had left me shaken.

This fraud ring was big, more far-reaching than I had imagined. Now I had serious questions about how many and who could be involved. Had I put my family at risk? I made what I hoped sounded like a little joke to Agent Schaefer about the possibility of the Witness Protection Program for me and my teenagers, but I was only half-joking.

But before we'd finished our conversation, I got a call from the buyers. "We had a courier deliver your payment for the appraisal," they told me, "but you left before he got there." And they asked if I'd head back to the property to meet him and pick up the check.

When I opened the envelope with the payment, I found a check made out to me from – of all things – a used car dealer in North Kansas City, Missouri. More than a little interesting! In time we'd learn that the leader of the fraud ring actually owned this dealership, and used it as a front for money laundering.

But for today, I'd done the deed, gotten paid, and the FBI had a record. We were underway.

I went back to my office to work on the appraisal report, and wound up inventing the rationale to bump a house worth $700,000 to $1,473,000.

Though I went ahead with what was expected, my fears for my family gnawed at me and demanded a response.

I called my kids' mother and tried to explain without giving away everything what was going on. She agreed to invite them to camp out at her house for the next couple of weeks. Though this arrangement created some inconveniences for them, it helped calm some of my fears. If, say, someone was watching our house, they wouldn't be targets. Who knew for sure what all this was going to mean? I wasn't taking chances with my children.

Syncing the Appraisals

In a couple of days I got a surprise call from the second appraiser working on the house. "Don," he said, "we've got work to do. I've read your report, but the highest I can bump the value is $1.2 million. We've got about a $300,000 variance in our reports to account for."

I wanted to say, "You're okay to lie about the value of that house to the tune of $500,000, but you won't do it for $800,000?"

But I just provided a pause I hoped he'd interpret as my mulling over his dilemma, then agreed to change my report to match his $1.2 million value. Really, what's $300,000 between two cheating appraisers when none of the numbers is close to correct anyway? Easiest appraisal value adjustment I ever made!

My friends at the FBI were now alert to opportunities, so they asked if I'd drop off the completed appraisal to the mortgage company in person, rather than faxing it in.

"We'd like to see if we can find out all we can about those other properties the realtor mentioned – like addresses, or where these deals stand. So when you go in, would you direct the conversation? And record it?"

Maybe at last I was actually going to "wear a wire." As it turned out, I was handed a small recorder to tuck in my breast pocket. And I did as instructed at the mortgage company, asking questions and looking for ways to poke for information without arousing suspicion. But I came away empty-handed; there was no eagerness to disclose insider stuff to an appraiser they didn't know well. "Probably smart if what you're doing is illegal," I thought to myself.

The arrests

Three weeks after this episode, when life felt like it was close to returning to normal, I got a call from the second appraiser involved in the deal. His voice sounded tense and a little scared.

"Have you heard what's going on?" he asked.

Total innocence on this end. "What do you mean?" I asked.

"I got a call today from the FBI! They made an appointment to talk with me about mortgage fraud!"

So the case was ready to move forward. "Thanks for the heads up," I said, trying to sound surprised and as concerned as he was. But as I hung up, I thought, "Sucks to be you..."

A few hours later, I'd hear from Agent Schaefer. The FBI had stopped the closing, then agents drove to the homes of the parties involved and announced to each that they were under investigation for mortgage fraud.

Boom!

"Don't speak with anyone from the fraud ring if they or their lawyers contact you," Agent Schaefer instructed me. "Next step will be the hearing of the evidence before a Grand Jury in a couple of weeks, on January 4, 2007."

He asked if I could plan to be there after lunch to testify. And there'd be a meeting before the trial with Linda Marshall Parker, the Department of Justice Assistant US Attorney prosecuting the case. "She'll walk you through what to expect," Agent Schaefer explained, "so you'll feel ready to tell your story."

News flash. I had no idea how I'd ever feel ready to tell my story in a federal courtroom in front of a grand jury. But I said little and thanked him for all the information. Christmas was coming in a week – then New Year's. Maybe the busyness of the holidays would distract me from this odd and threatening experience ahead.

If we were successful, the grand jury would hand down eleven indictments and charge these people with federal crimes. If we weren't successful, the defendants' attorneys would know I'd informed as soon as I testified; my "cover" would be blown. I had no idea what happened after that.

Grand Jury

I started the day on January 4, 2007 as normally as I could – with two appraisals, followed by a swing by the house to change to a suit and tie. "I look like I'm headed to a funeral," I told myself as I worked on wrangling the tie into place. "Hope it won't end up being mine."

But success was ours. After an hour's testimony I left the courthouse, but before I reached my house radio reports were breaking that the federal grand jury had handed down indictments of eleven people, including the Jackson County Executive and her lawyer husband. I flipped on the television as soon as I entered the house; all the local TV stations were broadcasting the news, too.

On to trial?

Initially the trial was set for February 2007 but because of the mayoral election intervening, it was rescheduled for June. As it turned out, Ms. Shields lost the election, receiving only 1.5% of the vote. It likely didn't help her campaign that the day her television ads debuted she was indicted for mortgage fraud.

I went back to work. My part in this case was finished. Now we just needed to see how it played out, and that was out of my hands. The appraiser had just officially established himself as an FBI informant, and it felt damn good.

CHAPTER THREE

CANCER IN THE SYSTEM, PART I

After the grand jury verdict calling for indictments broke to the media, newspaper and broadcast reporters jumped in with a fury. Prominent public figures, one running for mayor, had been charged with a felony by the Department of Justice. Enough "probable cause" existed to show that a crime had likely been committed and that Ms. Shields and her husband, and their collaborators, committed it. A trial would follow in a few months.

A couple of weeks after news of the indictments broke, a local political cartoonist decided to use the news as fodder for his work. The cartoon in the Kansas City Star showed the seller standing behind a podium with a "Shields for Mayor" sign on the front, and saying, "Why shouldn't I run...I've got a local following." And behind her stood three serious types in black suits with briefcases labeled "Prosecutors," "FBI Agents" and "Grand Jury." The incongruity of a standing indictment leveled against someone campaigning to lead our city wasn't lost on many.

The information I had provided was useful in getting the indictment, but much more evidence existed, too. The FBI and Department of Justice had documented numerous acts of real estate and mortgage fraud over the past few years. But our case served a unique purpose. The massive overprice and the prestigious address made for engaging copy. And because I'd called Agent Jensen before the transaction had been completed, we had actual recordings of the crime in process.

I learned later that most of the evidence in mortgage fraud was naturally historical. What is the FBI going to do? Uncover suspected criminal acts, then bug everyone suspected for months to see which transactions are planned as fraudulent?

Linda Parker Marshall, the Department of Justice attorney who prosecuted the case had explained that mortgage fraud doesn't take a completely predictable path; you can go about it various ways. So guessing ahead of time which of these paths potential criminals will choose or design is nearly impossible. But in this case we had real-time, in-process criminal activity on tape.

A new jury

My name didn't show up in the media reports as an FBI informer. I'd been promised anonymity until the case went to trial, partly as protection for me in case we hadn't uncovered criminal activity. There'd be no retribution from anyone if the information I gave didn't prove valuable. That's why I was surprised when a call came from Connie Swafford, President of the Kansas Mortgage Brokers' Association. Would I speak to a group of area bankers and mortgage brokers about mortgage fraud?

The lunch meeting was less than a month away; surely they planned their programs farther out than this. But the media blitz around the Shields case had pushed these groups into greater public scrutiny. Now the media and others had begun asking for interviews, digging for more information.

I knew I wasn't being invited because of my involvement with the FBI; no one knew about that except my family. I'd been suggested, I learned, because I was known for subprime mortgage review work, so these mortgage funding professionals must have figured that like an IRS auditor, I'd know something about how bad mortgages take place. The meeting was scheduled for February 8, 2007 three weeks away.

When I finished the call, I felt a mix of excitement and fear in equal measure.

The guy who loves what he does was jazzed. Reviewing appraisals and loan documents is fairly isolating and tedious, and at times what I found left me disgusted and sometimes a little powerless.

Hundreds of thousands of these loans were supported by appraisers who weren't telling the truth about the properties. At first I thought the errors were mistakes; maybe these men and women just didn't know how to complete an appraisal. But before long I began to see egregious mistakes too big to simply be a calculation or research or measurement error. Or I'd see a pattern of "mistakes" coming from one appraiser.

I rejected the appraisals, of course, and alerted the lenders about the issues. And without enthusiasm, I often filed a complaint against the offending appraiser with our licensing board. An investigation into their work would result. Part of me rebelled against what felt like being forced into a "whistleblower" role for my own profession, but another part took pride in what I did. And it wasn't just about me. I knew thousands of appraisers were saying "no" to lying; they deserved to know that they weren't alone. In this reviewer role, I could stand up for us. That felt good.

Of course I also knew some of these fraudulent appraisals were being commissioned by mortgage brokers and the lenders they were working with. This fraternity was likely a mix of good guys and their bad guy counterparts. I wanted all of them to know someone was paying attention. If the attention garnered by the Shields case gave an opportunity to push for more consistently honest behavior, so be it. *"A little fear of God never hurt anyone,"* my Mother used to tell me.

Part of my passion came from knowing how the whole system worked together, and therefore knowing better than some where to look for scams. It had served me well that my dad had had a career in lending before coming to appraising, so how the pieces fit made sense to me.

I knew information that could be distilled into what I thought of as the "twelve steps of fraud for profit" – and I'd seen these in action. As I reviewed them, I thought of times and people who "smelled" of each. The sequence of events usually looked like this:

1. The investment scammer attracts an investor with get-rich-quick promises. The investor

agrees to let him buy a house and borrow money using his credit.

At one time a lawyer representing a 25-year-old who had filed bankruptcy hired me. The young man lived in an apartment, yet had been given loans on twenty-five houses that were to be investment properties. Not surprisingly, the loans went bad; the properties went into foreclosure. To clear his name, the young man sued the individuals involved. In the process of reviewing the appraisals, we were able to demonstrate fraud, and the bankruptcy was discharged.

2. The scammer finds a house to buy and works with a dishonest appraiser to value the house for more than it is worth.

    As I reviewed appraisals, I saw on a near-daily basis properties with inflated values. It appeared buyers, sellers, realtors and appraisers were all working together to create these inflated values.

3. The scammer then works with a dishonest loan broker to use the inflated appraisal, and phony documents to get a lender to lend more money than the house is worth.

Beginning in 2002, I got phone calls from lenders wanting me to appraise a house for a certain value before I'd even done the work. And if my appraisal didn't agree with the value they'd determined, they wouldn't pay for my work.

4. The scammer buys the house and gets the inflated loan in the name of the investor or "straw buyer" who is responsible for the loan if it goes bad.

   Friends of my parents purchased an investment house in a deal too good to be true. "You'll put no money down," they were told, "and the property is already rented out so that rental will cover your payments." All they needed to do was put up their credit. There were no renters, and they ended up losing the house in this "get rich quick" scheme.

5. The scammer siphons money out of the inflated loan proceeds, often as "management fees." But the fees are not reflected on closing documents sent to the lender and investor, and so they may never know about them.

While doing appraisal reviews, I came across a Kansas City builder who was selling houses when no one else seemed to be able to, and for a lot more money than others were getting. As it turned out, the builder's brother-in-law was an appraiser, and his brother was a mortgage lender. So they teamed up to create a profitable scam. Two went to jail.

6. The investor is told the mortgage payments will be covered by rent paid by a tenant. But the rent can't keep pace with the oversize mortgage payments.

I knew a case in which investors had been told the houses they were buying would rent for $800 a month – and not told that reasonable rent would only be $500-$600 a month. When reality hit, rental income couldn't cover the investors' payments, and they lost the properties.

7. The loan goes into default and the lender forecloses to recoup some of its losses.

It wasn't unusual for a lender to loan, say, $250,000 on a property. Later, when they had to foreclose, the property might be worth only $175,000. Then, adding in the cost of repairing, *holding and managing, and reselling the property, the lender might lose $100,000 on such a loan.*

8. The straw buyer now stands to lose all his investment and faces a lawsuit by the lender.

    When lenders foreclosed on houses, they'd then sue the borrower for the difference between the size of the loan and the value at foreclosure. The borrower not only loses the property, but winds up in debt, and very often bankruptcy followed.

9. Tenants get evicted.

    These tenants had paid deposits and paid their rent on time. But because the investor owning the house had quit making payments to the lender, and therefore lost the property, tenants paid the price, even though they'd done nothing wrong.

10. Meanwhile, the scammer may list the inflated sale on the Multiple Listing Service where legitimate appraisers and real estate brokers use it to value other houses for sale. So buyers of those homes also end up paying too much.

In Midtown Kansas City, people were buying houses for $15,000-$20,000, put $10,000 into repairs on them – and then show them on the Multiple Listing Service for sale at $35,000 and sold for $75,000. These homes were sold, but deceptively from one investor to another in order to build up false sale numbers, and then use these false numbers as comparable to get their homes listed on the MLS at inflated prices.

11. County tax assessors may also relay on the inflated values of the homes to set tax assessment rates and so they over charge property owners on their property taxes.

Tax assessments work with average sales prices in an area, so when prices are artificially inflated, the value of other homes in the area are falsely inflated too. Assessments of value are skewed for all.

12. As more homes go into foreclosure, lenders, fearful of losing more money, tighten lending policies making it harder for people to get loans in the future.

That's why in 2008 the economy tanked, and now new homes loan are more difficult to get.

Plenty to talk to mortgage bankers about!

Clearly, I'd seen enough and been privy to enough of the pain caused by these double-dealings that I had plenty to say. But along with the passion, I felt a little fear.

Me presenting to a bunch of banker types? Up to now, the largest group I'd ever spoken to consisted of ten people. Plus, because of ADIID, I was that kid in school who never wanted to be up front unless he was clowning around. When things are happening too fast, and ideas and instructions have become a bunch of noise instead of something intelligible to respond to, you learn pretty quickly not to raise your hand to speak. It will not end well.

In the end, the chance to make life easier for my colleagues who did right won out and I agreed to speak. How bad could it be, after all? This time I knew my stuff, and with the Grand Jury testimony behind me I knew I could focus well enough to tell the story accurately. Nothing to lose, and a potential gain that mattered.

The FBI agreed to the presentation, but cautioned me about any mention of our case, since it had yet to go to trial, but that was no problem. I wasn't being invited for my connection to the case, just for my years of experience as a reviewer.

Plus, as it turned out, February 8 was my son's 16th birthday. He was getting closer to launching into a life with new challenges. It was time for Dad to do the same.

CHAPTER FOUR

CANCER IN THE SYSTEM, PART II

A serious meeting needed a banker-looking suit, so I invited my daughter Rachel to go shopping. This 14-year-old knew her way around style, and if I made a geeky choice I knew I'd hear about it for a long time, so we headed to Men's Wearhouse.

It didn't take long to narrow the options in dark suits to two choices, though one cost twice as much as the other. "I'm getting the nicer one," I told her, "but I'm keeping it 'til I either get married or get buried in it."

We moved to the collection of ties, and as I held up one for her opinion, she said, "Dad. What's that big lump on your neck?"

I had no idea what she was talking about, so I moved to a mirror. Sure enough, a lump about the size of half a baseball was sticking out of my neck.

What was this? My neck had been normal when I'd shaved just a few hours ago.

I was more confused than concerned. Healthy guy, no signs of illness. It couldn't be anything too cataclysmic, but I agreed to stop by an emergency room on the way home to be sure. I'd had sinus surgery a few weeks before and I wondered if it could be an infection from that episode. The emergency room physician agreed with my diagnosis and prescribed antibiotics. "If it doesn't go away in a couple of weeks," he advised, "you should probably see an ENT."

Three weeks later, the lump hadn't shrunk, so I followed the doctor's advice and scheduled with an Ear, Nose and Throat specialist. After chest x-rays and blood work, he didn't seem overly concerned. "Your tests turned out fine," he told me, "but in cases like this we usually order a biopsy. We don't want to miss anything."

That seemed reasonable, so the next day I completed two appraisals then drove myself to an outpatient clinic. No need to bother anyone else; I'm a turned-out-to-be-nothing kind of patient, so I was sure I could drive myself home.

But when I woke up from the anesthetic, my friend Kelly was sitting next to me. "What are you doing here?" I asked groggily. "How did you even know I was here?"

"You listed me as your Emergency Contact," she smiled. But then the smiled faded. "I need to get your doctor," she said, and left for a moment.

The doctor was direct. "Don," he began, "it turns out during the biopsy, some of your lymph nodes looked irregular. I removed six of them to check to be sure there's no cancer."

As if he hadn't just dropped the "C" word, he went on. "Biopsy results will be back in two to four days, so we'll know more then," he said. "And I've scheduled you for a PET scan on February 8."

Since this moment back in 2007 I've gotten to know many people who heard this same news from their doctors. It seems for most of us, reactions are fairly predictable.

As it was for me, it's nearly impossible to hear the word "cancer," even if it's used tentatively and inconclusively, without feeling like a death sentence was just handed down. I wonder now if I'd have reacted differently if Rachel and Daniel weren't so dependent on me. Who's to know? All I know is the next four days were the longest of my life.

When the call came, my heart sank. It appeared to be Non-Hodgkins Lymphoma, the doctor told me. We'd know more in a week or so after the PET scan, and generate a treatment plan with that information.

Telling the kids

Life crises are pretty self-revealing, I've learned. And what I saw was this: when threatened, I move quickly to the worst-case scenario and prepare to face it. Once I've stared the worst right in the eyes, anything that happens seems manageable.

So without a thought, I knew at once I had to tell the kids, to get them ready for whatever might be ahead. I grabbed my coat and drove to the high school where Rachel was playing in a basketball game. It wasn't like I had a plan. I just knew that we'd need to do this one together, as we did everything.

Rachel was between games when I came into the gym; she ran over to ask what I'd heard from the doctor. This wasn't the time or place, I knew, but she needed to hear something from me.

"We'll go out to dinner after your game," I told her, "and talk about it all."

Fortunately she was called away right then, so I joined her mother in the bleachers. Telling my ex-wife the bad news seemed to make sense to me. If, indeed, a worst-case scenario lay ahead for us, she'd be impacted too.

As soon I finished sharing what I knew, Daniel flashed into my mind. He'd need to be part of the dinner conversation, too, but he was probably at home by now. "I'm going after Daniel," I told my ex-wife, and left quickly.

Daniel had come straight home after school, and in a moment I would learn why. It turned out he already knew I had cancer; he was simply waiting for me to get the news.

"Daniel, how…?"

"Remember that conference on medicine I was invited to in Arizona last year? We talked about cancer diagnosis. And I learned there that if it takes four days instead of two to get your test results, it means they've found the bad stuff and are staging and grading the cancer. I've known all weekend, actually." And he went on to give an overview of what the treatment might look like ahead.

I didn't know what to feel. He'd known the outcome and carried it alone for two days. That's no load for a 15-year-old to bear and I hated that for him, but I also felt so proud of both his knowledge and his composure. Fifteen going on fifty in my eyes. I couldn't begin to process what he was outlining about the treatments; too much was coming in to barely hear him. But I knew now it would be our talk with Rachel, not just mine. We grabbed our coats and headed back to the gym.

Rachel was on the court when we came in the double doors, but she must have had one eye peeled in our direction because as soon as we entered, she left the game. No matter it was in the middle of a game! It turned out her mother had given her the news during a break, and she fell sobbing into my arms.

"We're gong to be okay, Rachel," I said quickly. "Now go back in there and finish this game!"

"Dad," she shook her head. "If you make me go out there, I'll just foul five times in a row and get thrown out."

"Then we'll save some poor girl from taking some terrible hits," I said with a wink. "You're done; let's go."

Dinner conversation that night was the most sober of our life together. I laid out what we knew, and we talked about what might lie ahead. Neither was interested in chirpy optimism. Like me, they took the hard stuff by facing the worst first. So we talked about what might happen if I died, about the right living situation and financial provision for them.

I would later learn this "facing the worst" approach was something counselors sometimes used because once clients faced the worst, anything less than that seemed more manageable. I didn't know we were doing family therapy; I just knew we had to find a way to move ahead together.

Beyond the family

I called the FBI office the next day, and told Agent Schaefer about the diagnosis. "Do you want me to tape my testimony, in case I'm not able to be part of the trial?" I asked.

"We have more than enough recordings of you to make the case," he responded quickly. "But Don, we really need you." I inferred from his tone that he meant more than just my usefulness as a witness. We'd gotten to know each other fairly well in the short time we had worked together, and it was clear to me a bond had formed.

A few days later I spoke at the mortgage bankers and brokers meeting; the response was lukewarm, but I wasn't offended. I knew so much these finance professionals didn't.

My work with the FBI and the DOJ attorneys had already alerted me to the possibilities of far-reaching rumblings in the world of mortgage securities and the countless fraud rings that were at work. The audience looked prosperous, secure, and stable. It might not be long before their world would be as rocked as mine had been when I received the news about cancer.

As I left the meeting and drove to my PET scan to find out about the cancer in my system, it occurred to me that the folks I just left had their own cancer eating away at a national and international system millions relied on.

Cancer treatment

There would be three rounds of chemotherapy, the doctor told me. In a silly twist it happened that the doctor and I recognized each other – our sons had shared a first-period class at school. The news he delivered about the number of treatments didn't please me, so I covered my reaction with a joke. "Hey!" I said. "Just remember, we're in the same neighborhood and I know where you live. These had better not be too bad!"

We both laughed, but inside I wasn't laughing. What would it mean to have these quantities of poison coming into my body? What really was ahead here?

When I went for my first treatment, I had little idea what to expect. Would I be in a little hospital room alone? Most likely. My mental picture couldn't have been farther off. The chemo room had about 60 patients, all seated in large recliners and hooked up to bags of chemicals.

The intervention looked the same for all of us; that's where the similarity ended. We were young, old, male, female, black, brown, white, healthy-looking, and barely upright.

During the first treatment, I'd asked how long I'd be at the center, and was told about 3 hours. So, I naively scheduled an appraisal for 3-1/2 hours after the treatment was to begin. At the three-hour mark, I called to the nurse to unhook the apparatus and began to gather my things. "Mr. Gossman, your chemo bag isn't empty. You'll be here a bit longer." It was a first-heads up that life was no longer on my schedule.

The hardest part of the treatment episodes was the waiting. Waiting to be called in. Waiting for the nurses to prepare the chemo concoction. Waiting for hours while the drugs ran into my body. Waiting to feel sick and exhausted. But after the first episode, I reset expectations, and tried to breathe. It was a strategy that would serve me well.

The particular cocktail designed for my kind of cancer would cause my hair to fall out, I was told. Drat! It was a credit to genes and nothing more, I knew, but I'd had some pride in being that middle-aged guy who still had a head full of dark, thick, wavy hair. No more.

When my hair started to go, the kids and I decided to get there first, and I invited them to shave my head. Now remember these are two teenagers with a pair of clippers, so the head shave moved first to a fairly dramatic Mohawk. After a serious application of gel and far too many photos for Facebook they agreed to finish the job, and leave my head shining. It occurred to me later that this interlude of silliness had helped all three of us to feel less like victims and more like ourselves. A little time out during a trek through uncertainty.

After the chemo, fifteen radiation treatments followed. In this phase, I was fitted for a half-body cast made of plastic mesh, form-fitted to my body from my elbows to the top of my head. The contraption was tight enough that I couldn't lick my lips, twitch my nose, or blink my eyes. Then they bolted me to the treatment table so my body was locked in place. The radiation machine began moving around my head and neck; I could smell my flesh frying as the machine did its work.

I quickly saw I was going to have to get control of my emotions or these treatments would be unbearable. I'd heard of others who had to be sedated to endure them; now I understood why. So I worked on relaxing. I'd picture walking on a beautiful beach with Rachel and Daniel, a cool breeze touching our faces, the crunch of sand under out feet, the splash of waves hitting the shore nearby. It worked.

I had been told I'd need about three weeks of treatments. Since I had signed up for five days a week on the table, I did the math and concluded I'd be finished after fifteen episodes. So sure was I that I scheduled myself into a corporate meeting in Phoenix right after the fifteenth session concluded. Unfortunately, the medical staff saw it differently. When I was leaving after Session Twelve, I mentioned to the nurse how glad I was to only have three more of these to go. "What do you mean?" she responded. "You're to have eighteen treatments, not fifteen." I waved her off. "I'm pretty sure fifteen is what I thought I signed up for," I said. "I'm sure that'll do it."

The doctor got word of my self-prescribing bent, and let me know I needed the full protocol of eighteen. When I pushed back, he said, "Fine. We can stop at fifteen. But in that case, be ready in six months to come back for another round of fifteen." I went on the trip, and finished the course when I returned.

As it turned out, however, those last three treatments were by far the hardest. I found my throat nearly swollen shut so I could barely swallow, and could eat no solid food. Radiation shut down my sense of taste temporarily, but killed the salivary glands on the right side permanently.

Lessons

When I went to the first chemo treatment, I purposely refused help from those who offered, and went alone. Somehow facing this by myself seemed heroic or something; I'm not sure to this day. But soon others refused to accept my decision to make the experience a solo act.

For example, without asking me, my friend Lori organized the parents of the kids I'd coached in soccer and softball into bringing us meals. I felt awkward receiving them, and a little guilty that I couldn't care for my family by myself. But in the warmth and graciousness of these friends, those feelings soon changed. They weren't pitying or judging me; they were caring for us in a time of need, just as I would have cared for them.

Three months after I began, chemo and radiation were behind me. And so far as anyone could tell, so was the spread of the cancer. But as I got ready to re-enter life more fully, I could see something big had shifted inside me.

In reality, I hadn't had a death-defying encounter with illness; but in the beginning for all I knew, death might well be the outcome. And in those very long hours waiting for chemicals to drip into my arm, and those segments bolted to the radiation treatment table, I thought about my life as I hadn't before.

What if this had been the end? And if not this, what if something else was ahead that might mark the end before I expected it to come? What would I want to say I had lived for? What did I want to leave behind?

It was about Rachel and Daniel, of course. They are life to me, and living for their best had consumed me up to now. But what did I want for them? Just physical care, good jobs, happy homes? All these, yes. But I began to understand how deeply I wanted more. I wanted a world for them where good guys win and bad guys don't, where the values I held close would be reinforced.

The question was, how could I help? I'm not Gandhi or Martin Luther King. Little by little it became clearer that the work I was doing to quell mortgage fraud could be a contribution. It wouldn't change everything, but it could change something. It could help make one small place in their world more honest, more true.

I'd testify in front of a federal grand jury, of course, but now my determination was different. That one act wasn't going to be enough. I didn't know how, but I would do more. And now that I had had the privilege of looking death in the eye, I felt fearless.

Even if there were costs to me – and there would have to be, even though I couldn't know what they'd be – I was going to contribute. I could, and I would. *How* would take care of itself. It appeared we'd killed the cancer in my system; it was time now to move with the same determination against cancers in the financial system.

Meanwhile, back at the trial...

The trial had been scheduled for June 2007 but the defense asked for and received a five-month delay until November 2007.

We heard that one of their concerns was the sympathy that might be aroused in the jury if I showed up to testify without hair because of cancer treatments. Someone else suggested they'd delayed because they were hoping I'd die, and not be able to give evidence against them. Of course the tapes of our conversations were solidly in the possession of the FBI, so I thought that suggestion was a stretch.

But if it took a year for the trial to convene I was ready. For me, a fight for justice was underway.

THE CRISIS IN COFFEYVILLE

When the cancer treatments concluded, I was ready to refocus on work. Fortunately, the appraisal group I worked with was growing. A banner year lay ahead so it appeared our good reputations in the banking community were serving us well.

As mid-year approached, I got pulled into helping in a crisis that – to my relief – had nothing to do with secretly recording anybody who might potentially have connections to the mafia!

On June 30th following a six-inch downpour, the Verdigris River in southern Kansas overflowed its banks and flooded the Coffeyville Oil Refinery. The refinery scrambled to close down operations before the floodwaters could cover their complex, but in their haste, someone left the valve on an oil tank open.

Over 7,500 barrels of oil spilled out. As a result, when the floodwaters engulfed the town of Coffeyville, 440 houses and lots, as well as 75 businesses were not only underwater, but also covered in oil. A double dose of decimation.

The refinery could foresee their company tied up in a class action lawsuit filed by Coffeyville homeowners and businesses for the next 10-15 years – and they wanted the homeowners to move along with their lives as soon as possible. So they chose instead to offer victims of the spill a buyout at 110% of the value of their properties, as they would have been appraised the day before the flood. And in order to make such an offer, they needed appraisals of the homes and businesses that had been impacted.

So, our company got a call from the refinery's attorney wanting to know how many appraisals we could complete in a week's time in Coffeyville, Kansas.

Now, here was a new one for us! First, I had to determine just where Coffeyville, Kansas was and discovered it was located not far from the Kansas/Oklahoma border, and prided itself on being the location where the infamous Dalton Gang met its end. Because of my own recent ventures into criminal apprehension, I thought immediately work in this location would fit pretty well!

But another first lay ahead. The company needed 440 homes and lots appraised in a very short time frame. Not only would this assignment entail a larger quantity of homes than I'd worked with before, but I'd never appraised oil-damaged homes. Also, not being familiar with Coffeyville wasn't just a geography lesson. In my business, determining accurate comparables to use in appraising is easier if you've done business there and you know the real estate market intimately.

But this felt like a welcome challenge after my bout with cancer. I assured the client I'd become familiar with the specifics of appraising oil damage and engaged two local appraisers to provide the local experience and perspective my team would need to be sure our values were accurate.

Besides these two, I lined up three appraisers from my office and two contract appraisers. The six of us met at 5:30 am in the parking lot of our office, and drove the 2-1/2 hours to Coffeyville. We talked on the way about what we might expect to see; none of us were adequately prepared for the view that opened to us as we drove into town. Twelve blocks of the town were decimated by flood damage, and coated with oil.

Since the railroad had sustained considerable damage to their operation, too, they'd brought in a large crew for their clean up. To house them, the railroad purchased the only hotel left in town that wasn't oil-damaged, so we'd be staying an hour away in Bartlesville, Oklahoma.

Checking in with employees of the Pilot Cat Corporation, which had been hired by the Refinery to oversee the recovery effort, I learned we had three months to complete the appraisals. There'd be no time to lose.

So we jumped in and completed our first 75 inspections, a hot, smelly, messy job in the midst of a Kansas scorcher, and oil ranging from 1-8 feet high on both the outside and inside of the homes.

When we finished these, I met with Oland Roberson from Pilot Cat to report we'd be working up the first portion of the appraisals over the next week, but that there'd be a week's delay before the second portion would begin. We needed to start working up the first group and have them reviewed by the lawyers and I had scheduled a vacation with my children to the Grand Cayman Island. "I've just survived a battle with cancer," I explained to Oland,

"and our family has been through a lot. I'm not going to miss this time with my children for anything."

As it turned out, Oland's son had just battled cancer himself, so my request was received with understanding and support.

Five weeks later we completed work on the 440 residential properties – seven weeks ahead of our deadline. Getting a job done well and ahead of schedule always felt good to me, but this time these results meant even more. As soon as the appraisals came in, homeowners had the information they needed to decide about settling a claim with Coffeyville Resources, collect the settlement, and move on with their lives.

In the end, 438 of the 440 homeowners ended up settling in a matter of months. Only twenty-eight homeowners appealed our valuation – of these, 15 were kept the same, and only 13 were changed. We saw a 94% acceptance of our appraised values as a mark of significant success.

But the real success to me didn't rest in a professional accomplishment – even though this was a big one in my industry. It was much more about all these homeowners having this disaster behind them, and recovery ahead.

Maybe I was sharing with them my relief at having my own personal cancer "disaster" behind me; I wasn't sure. But using my expertise to help others find better days felt good.

I went back to Kansas City to prepare for the Federal Trial where I was to be the opening witness for the Federal Government. It occurred to me that heading to the trial felt a lot like the drive to Coffeyville. Who knew exactly what this challenge meant?

I couldn't have imagined the degree or complexities of life changes that testimony in court would bring for my family and me.

CHAPTER SIX

THE TRIAL

T he jury was to be seated on Monday morning, November 6, 2007 with opening statements scheduled for that morning, so the US Attorney asked me to be at the Federal Court House at 1 pm. But when I arrived I was told the morning's first task of jury selection hadn't been completed.

After the Grand Jury indictment, some in the local media had suggested the case might be a political witch-hunt by the new US Attorney's office because the defendants' Democratic leanings differed from the administration's Republican stance. So, because of the publicity around the case, the jury pool was larger than normal and selection was going slowly.

I waited in the witness room for four hours to find out that, by day's end, we'd gotten no farther than jury selection and opening arguments.

"That's enough for today," the judged ruled. "We will reconvene tomorrow at 9 am."

Uncovering a fraud ring

I wasn't privy to the opening arguments, but that evening in thinking about the trial, I reviewed what I guessed my friends on the prosecution team might have said as they introduced their evidence for not just a fraudulent real estate sale, but an entire fraud ring operating in the city.

I had learned from early conversations with the FBI and others that one of my colleagues – a fellow review appraiser – helped uncover the existence of a whole series of fraudulent transactions. His suspicions were aroused when information about a purchase didn't make sense.

In his case, he looked at a home that appraised and sold for $450,000. However, said property had actually been an MLS listing for 16 months previously, with the price steadily dropping from the initial list price of $374,500. On January 1, 2006 it had finally hit a low of just $260,000 before being taken off the market. *Yet just three days later, on January 4, it sold for nearly $200,000 more than the asking price just a few days earlier.*

No seller gets this lucky! So the appraisal reviewer decided to dig deeper, spurred on by the fact that a quick check showed that the buyer in this case had recently purchased not just this one, but actually seven properties that left him with over $2 million in loans. That's a lot of money to be able to borrow!

In time he would uncover more than forty home purchases as questionable as these. They included properties that had all been taken off the market then relisted within days for significantly higher amounts. And on the recorded documents the same notary's name appeared. Something was very wrong.

In simple fraud involving one home loan, the bad guy is usually the borrower. The down payment might have been borrowed, contrary to what he reported to the lender, or other debt that might have disqualified him from getting the loan might have been covered up. Income information might have been altered.

But in big time fraud for profit, the bad guy is usually an industry professional.

Agent Jensen reported that 80% of losses reported involved collaboration by industry insiders. These often involved multiple loans and institutions, and participants are usually paid to play. The borrower might not even be aware of the scheme he's become a part of.

In the Shields case, the homebuyers told the mortgage company that: (1) they had a combined monthly income of $37,800; (2) that they owned three properties, and (3) they had a $216,000 savings account.

In reality, these lies were so big I had to marvel at their boldness! An income of $37,800 a month? A mortgage loan broker on the take just pulled that figure out of the blue. Owning only three properties? In reality, the buyers were owners of ten properties; that's a mountain of debt that would scare any lender. And that savings account? Non-existent.

So, the investigation of this ring was solidly underway. And when I made those recordings of my conversations with the loan processor, buyers' real estate agent and the second appraiser, the FBI was able to observe one of these schemes while it unfolded, collecting evidence nearly as quickly as it was being created.

We were on the trail of people who were lining their pockets – and richly so – with illegal profits from transactions that never should have happened.

The people who didn't go to trial

As it had turned out, after the case broke and the Grand Jury issued indictments, seven of the eleven people charged pleaded guilty. Along with the man who organized this ambitious scheme, these included the homebuyers, the real estate agent I'd met that day when I appraised the house, the title agent, a crooked CPA and a "henchman" who filled in gaps in the caper.

The organizer of the scheme got a ten-year prison sentence and was on the hook for $5.6 million in restitution. The title agent and the CPA went to prison, as well. The "henchman," and my colleague the appraiser got probation, though they came away with requirements to pay restitution. The appraiser also lost his license. The realtor fled the country to Iran before he could be sentenced, so a federal warrant for his arrest still exists.

The mortgage loan broker, the closer for the title company and the two sellers all opted to go to trial instead of pleading guilty, so it would be these four I'd face tomorrow.

Another sleepless night ensued. I'd been an expert witness in federal court before, but never when the stakes of the case were as high as this, and my testimony might make as much difference as it could this time.

On the stand

The next morning, I was the first witness on the stand for the prosecution. I scanned the gathering. To my right were the jurors; on my left the US Federal judge and court reporter. The prosecutors' table had two FBI agents, Assistant US Attorneys and their support staff. The audience consisted of reporters from newspapers, television and radio stations.

The four defendants, their three lawyers and three assistants huddled around the defense table.

Linda Parker Marshall, US Attorney, stepped up to question me, and began by explaining how I became part of the case, then asked me to tell my story. Two hours later, the defense attorneys took over. The first chose an aggressively adversarial line of questioning, and went after my ethics and motives.

My head told me to keep calm; he was just trying to get me upset so I'd say something stupid. But my gut wasn't listening, and on two occasions the judge warned me to limit my answers to the questions asked.

The second defense attorney grilled me for an hour, but without as much edge. Number three turned out to be their kinder, gentler team member, who remarked about my good reputation. Was this some "Good Cop, Bad Cop" routine, I wondered.

After four hours on the stand, I stepped down, adrenalin pumping, but exhausted. My part, over. Now other arguments would proceed, and the jury would decide.

After 8 more days of testimony, followed by four days of deliberation, the jury came back with two guilty and two not-guilty verdicts.

Guilty? The loan broker and title company closer, both facing prison sentences.

But even though eleven of the jurors voted to convict the sellers as participants in the scheme, one hold out kept their decision from being unanimous, and the sellers were acquitted. The Kansas City Star ran a photo of them with their lawyers laughing their way down the courthouse steps. The headline read, "Free and Clear."

15 minutes of fame is plenty for me

The day the verdict was announced, I found myself referenced in a statement to the press issued by the US Attorney's Office:

"While much of the public attention regarding this case has focused on these two defendants, for the U.S.

Attorney's Office this case was about mortgage fraud. It is important to remember that the government did not seek out any particular defendants in this case. Instead, this case had its roots in the personal integrity of a private citizen - an honest appraiser who became suspicious and contacted an F.B.I. agent to voice his concerns."

They were, of course, trying to address criticisms that the charges had been politically motivated, and intended to set the record straight, to be sure the focus stayed on mortgage fraud.

Though the press reported the outcome of the trial, they never referenced the US Attorney's press release that made clear I'd come to them as an honest appraiser, not a suspect in the case who was trying to "cut a deal." I wouldn't see until much later how this omission would impact my business.

But after the press release, I got calls from the local FOX and NBC affiliates asking for interviews. I did both, but found they had little interest in discussing the harm done by overvaluing properties; it was the magnetic names involved in the case that drew attention.

My disgust at the direction of the conversation was mitigated, however, by the fact that my kids got to see me on TV. That counts for something with very-hard-to-impress teenagers.

I also got a call from the director of the Kansas Real Estate Appraisal Board, asking if I'd write an article for their newsletter about the case and what I'd learned, but I declined.

Enough of all this drama! After a year that combined the FBI, cancer and a federal court trial, I wanted the beautiful simplicity of normal. Nothing more.

Second thoughts

In January 2008 I would change my mind about writing the article when I read in the news that the defendants in the case were now suing the US government to recover their $200,000-plus legal defense costs! Their basis for the suit? They dusted off the "politically motivated" argument and put it front and center.

Seriously? I could feel my blood starting to boil at this arrogance.

Even if all I wanted now was for life to get back to normal, I had to speak out. And the Real Estate Appraisal Board had offered me a forum with 1,000 appraisers, so I put together my experience, with a clear view to pushing for more integrity in our profession, and sent it off. The article got enough visibility that a national newsletter with a readership of 65,000 in the mortgage industry asked to reprint it.

After the article came out in March 2008 my email blew up with over 100 messages from across the country. There were kudos like these:

"Thank you for 'standing tall.'"

"You make me proud to be an appraiser."

"As a banker for twenty years and an appraiser for 45, I thank you for what you did for all of us, not just appraisers, but the public as a whole."

But the messages that meant more were those expressing pride and renewed hope in our profession.

"You give hope that during times like these, it means something to be a professional and not a 'vendor' of a commodity as those in the lending industry would like to say we are."

"What you did was costly to you in stress and time but to our profession it was invaluable. Your actions embellished my pride in the work we do."

"I hope if I am ever confronted with a similar situation to yours that I do the right thing."

I felt humbled and a little overwhelmed. Something about this unintentional impact seemed to bring some balance to the trauma my cancer diagnosis had imposed on my family. But even more, these people confirmed what I had believed: there were many more who wanted to do right than the deceivers out to manipulate our profession to make a quick buck.

Finding my voice

A couple of months after the article came out, the director of the Missouri Real Estate Board called, inviting me to speak at a regional meeting of real estate licensing officials coming up in July, 2008. Attendees would come from 31 states, and the meeting would feature a program that included both an FBI agent and the chief economist for the Federal Reserve Bank of St. Louis.

This one caught me off guard. Speaking? I'd done one speech the year before on appraisal fraud to that group of mortgage bankers in Kansas City. But that was before the notoriety around the trial ignited media attention, both for good and bad. How public was I really ready to go with this determination to help with the mortgage industry cleanup?

Besides, there was still inside me a kid with ADHD struggling through speaking assignments he couldn't avoid at school. Did I want to put that guy in front of a mike with more than 100 smart, well educated, and polished people in the audience?

There'd be no way to clown my way through mistakes with this crowd.

But once again, the cancer-induced determination to speak for the good won out and I agreed.

It occurred to me that they didn't need to hear someone with a PhD in macroeconomics. Sometimes change can be driven from the bottom up, by one man with a story and a message that is real. That I could do.

However, I was so new at this "professional presentation" stuff that I had no idea how to create the PowerPoint they requested. Fortunately, my daughter came to my rescue and left me with a slide show I couldn't believe.

The talk went well. I was interrupted by applause twice and following that experience, realtors' groups in the Arkansas Realtors' Association issued speaking invitations.

The informant was becoming an informer. I thought to myself, "Should be an interesting 2008."

I had no idea at the time how interesting – and how deeply devastating – 2008 and beyond would prove to be, not just for me, but also for millions of families and the American economy.

CHAPTER SEVEN

CHANGING THE SYSTEM

After years of fraudulent activity on the part of banks, lenders, brokers, realtors, appraisers and others, at last the mortgage-lending and securities s*** hit the fan.

On September 29, 2008, Dow Jones Index fell nearly 778 points, or almost 7%, the largest single-day point decline in history.

Like many others, I knew we were at the beginning of very dark days. Banks had made a trillion dollars of subprime loans from 2005-2008, and in this pool some 70% of the appraisals were inflated. If these appraisals were inflated only 20% - a number I thought realistic from all I'd seen - the result would be $140 billion in losses. And the problems didn't stop with subprime loans; both prime and FHA loans had been mishandled, too.

In the midst of this macroeconomic crisis, I was worried about my appraisal business. But my concerns came from threats that differed from those of my fellow appraisers.

Early in 2007 I'd quit working for myself and joined two other men in a franchise-structured appraisal business. They handled the commercial appraisals; I ran the residential side. As we moved ahead with our agreements, I'd alerted them about my work with the FBI, and though at that time none but federal agents knew my identity, my name could become public knowledge if after the trial there were convictions, as I was sure there would be. Both men assured me they were on board; it might even help our new business if the public knew how seriously we took ethics.

But after the trial, I began to hear rumblings that caused me concern. Some in mortgage lending – my potential clients – acknowledged my honesty, but were skittish about using me professionally for fear they might be "outed" for less-than-stellar practices.

And there was another twist. I learned that other lenders assumed that no one like me would inform on his profession unless he had done something illegal himself and had worked out a deal to trade information for immunity from prosecution.

The combination of these two perceptions drove away business. That, along with the downturn in real estate and lending activity driven by the dive in the economy began significantly cutting into my income.

Fortunately, I've always been a conservative guy and planned ahead for the inevitable ups and downs that come with any business like mine, so I hoped for a turnaround, or an economic turnover before my backup savings could no longer back me up.

Writing on the "Wall of Shame"

The mood at the October 2008 Kansas City Mortgage Bankers Association meeting I attended was somber, to put it mildly. During one of the breaks I connected with David Bowles, a senior risk manager with the mortgage securitizer Fannie Mae, who had given a solid tutorial on their view of the collapse happening around us. He included what he called a "Wall of Shame" – a collection of cheaters and crooks who had contributed to the System's breakdown.

I told him about my experience with the FBI and suggested another name for his Wall of Shame, the leader of the Kansas City mortgage fraud ring we had just taken down.

He wanted to know more, so I shared the article I'd written. Later I got a note telling me Fannie Mae intended to use the article as a training tool in their work with quality control appraisers at the Fannie Mae national underwriting center.

I was pleased and grateful. Fannie Mae was a huge player in the mortgage lending space. If Fannie Mae appraisal reviewers had a better handle on how appraisal fraud took place, the impact of our case might go beyond the world of appraisers; we'd have more support for doing right.

A date with Fannie

The following week, my part-time assistant buzzed me to say some lady named Fannie was on the phone. Did I want to take the call?

"Fannie" turned out to be Amy Heinz, Senior Industry Relations Manager for Fannie Mae's mortgage fraud program, inviting me to be part of a fraud-awareness presentation coming up in a few months in Las Vegas.

I said no. "I'm an appraiser," I explained. "Teaching like that – it's not what I do."

But she pushed back. "I'm just asking that you tell your story," she said. "And really, Don, if you don't get involved, how do we make sure it won't happen again?"

The woman should have been in sales; as soon as she appealed to my commitment to straightening out these sick systems, I was in.

Las Vegas, March 2009

The meeting was the 2009 Mortgage Bankers Association National Fraud Conference. Our session, billed as "Anatomy of a Sting," was one of the conference breakouts, and I was one of three professionals (the others represented a title company and a mortgage lender; both national companies) who had worked undercover with the FBI. Having the FBI label and "sting" description sounded more interesting than many of the other legal and technical sessions going on, so attendance and interest were high.

This audience intimidated me: people from Fannie Mae and Freddie Mac, representatives of the Departments of Treasury, Justice and Housing and Urban Development, as well as officials of 200 of the largest US banks.

"Good thing I'm just here to tell my story," I reminded myself. "This crowd could rattle me a little!"

After our presentation, Amy Heinz invited me to lunch with a group she called the "eleven most important people in the lending industry."

When Amy introduced me, I was a little taken aback to find the first question someone asked was, "Don, are you a Republican or a Democrat?" My politics mattered to these folks?

"I'm neither," I answered quickly. "I'm an American. It took both sides to screw this up, and it's going to take both sides to fix it." Case closed, and we went on to other topics.

But I took note of the intensity in my voice, and the anger in my chest as I answered.

Man! I felt strongly about this whole question of restoring integrity to a sick system. And maybe Amy was right about the need to speak out; if people like me didn't, what right did we have to complain?

I determined then I'd take other opportunities to tell my story if they presented themselves, whether I felt under qualified or not.

Maybe caring was a qualification I hadn't considered.

Denver, June 2009

When FBI Agent Schaefer called to invite me to present to the FBI's National Mortgage Fraud Team I saw a platform. There'd be about 70 FBI agents in attendance, he told me, along with 40 assistant US attorneys, and a number of fraud investigators from HUD's Office of the Inspector General. The conference was designed to provide guidelines to agents in the field as they investigated mortgage fraud.

My story could be a help to this gathering, I thought. Appraisers were part of the problem. This audience might help enforce regulations that kept us on the straight and narrow.

I called the session "Mortgage Fraud: An Insider's Perspective." I wasn't an insider committing fraud, but I was certainly an insider to how it was done, so I figured the title wasn't a stretch. And it was certainly more enticing than "101 Things You Need to Know About Appraisals."

When I arrived in Denver, I met an assistant US attorney from Kansas City, who prepped me for the audience, then encouraged me to get a good night's sleep. He'd meet me at 9:00 a.m. the next morning for bagels, and we'd go together to the Federal Courthouse for the conference. I thought, "Well, first, sleep isn't going to happen at all tonight, and second, I don't care for bagels." But I thanked him and we went our separate ways.

After presenting the facts about appraisal fraud, I launched into proposals for changes that could help keep appraisal fraud from happening. The five I thought could make the biggest difference, I explained, were these:

1. Appraiser independence. Lenders can't be allowed to put undue influence on appraisers to get the values of homes assigned as they wish.

2. Reasonable and customary fees. Since nearly all large banks owned their own appraisal management companies, they could charge the borrower $600 for appraisal, pay $200 for an appraisal, and pocket the difference as profit. Becoming an appraiser requires a college degree, 3000 hours of experience, and an additional 250 hours of classroom training. No one in his right mind would go through all that to make $24,000 a year, I explained. If we expected professionalism from appraisers, we needed to see that they were paid like professionals

3. Regulation of Appraisal Management Companies. AMCs were created originally because

lenders sometimes made loans to buyers outside their local area, and needed to acquire appraisals in places where they weren't familiar with the professionals. So AMCs hired a number of appraisers in different areas and served as their "middle man" to provide this service. But they were unregulated, so they were accountable to no one for the integrity of their reporting.

4. A Wall of Separation Between Appraisers and Lenders. I liked the way the VA handled this issue. They required each geographic lending area to have a roster of approved appraisers, and to use them on a rotating basis. Therefore no lender would be able to predict who the appraiser would be for the loan he was making.

5. A 33% Rule. This would mean that if a bank had its own Appraisal Management Company, only 1/3 of the appraisals they requested could be provided by that AMC. The rest would need to be farmed out to AMCs outside the bank, lessening the probability of insider cheating.

When I called for questions, there were many. But the most interesting to me came from National Fraud Task Force Director Travis Yarborough, who asked where I saw problems next appearing in mortgage lending.

I told him to expect these issues showing up in FHA loans. In 2006-2007 only 5% of loans were FHA; by 2009 45% of loans were FHA-backed. But regulations on how FHA loans are made hadn't changed for years. What was to keep the arena for fraud from simply shifting there?

I left the conference in a cab feeling quiet and satisfied; the beautiful summer day only reinforced my tranquility.

However, in the two hours between that cab ride and boarding the plane, a sudden storm dumped a foot of hail on the runways, and we wound up being evacuated from the plane and herded into bathrooms for safety since a tornado had been spotted west of the airport.

Some inner voice I wanted badly to ignore suggested this radical change in weather might be giving me cosmic warnings about the future. I decided to ignore the voice, but headed for the plane feeling more sober than I had three hours before.

My warnings about FHA loans made a difference

It appeared the inner voice had been wrong. Three months after the conference, a letter from the

Department of Housing and Urban Development went to banks, warnings them about the need for accurate appraisals when making FHA-backed loans, The letter used some of the same language and points I had made in the Denver presentation.

At first, I felt gratified.

However, it was quickly apparent that since there were no penalties meted out to lenders that didn't comply, they would ignore the letter. Clearly, punishments were going to be required to enforce this call to honesty.

Denver, May 2010

When I got the call to present in May of 2010 to the Financial Institution Fraud Unit of the FBI in Denver, I saw a chance to push again for new, stiffer regulations to an audience of FBI Agents who focused on mortgage fraud.

I will admit, the kid in me was a little jazzed about just being in the room with nearly 100 FBI agents. My brothers and I used to watch a TV series about the FBI on Sunday nights. Now one of the Gossman boys was heading out to teach them something. Who would have guessed it?

The session focused on how to commit fraud in an appraisal report – right up my alley. For each of the nine sections of an appraisal report, I gave five questions the agents could use to determine if any information had been falsified.

I knew some in the audience had thought of appraisers like a smart-ass tee shirt slogan I'd seen at a convention. It read: *"Appraiser: Someone who does precision guesswork based on unreliable data provided by those of questionable knowledge. See also: wizard, magician."*

So most importantly, I wanted to make clear appraisals weren't just opinions; they were fact-based, and black-and-white. Opinions can't be prosecuted, so agents needed to see for themselves we worked in facts, not hunches.

By the session's end, I don't think anyone questioned the authority of the work we did. So now I could seize the opportunity to again make the case for the only real solutions I saw: new rules to assure appraiser independence.

Columbia, South Carolina, February 2011

All this work came to a head for me about nine months later when I was asked in early 2011 to teach at a Mortgage Fraud Seminar at the Department of Justice's National Advocacy Center, the Office of Legal Education for United States Attorneys. This facility trains about 10,000 DOJ prosecutors every year; they asked me to explain how appraisal fraud is committed and how to spot it.

Previous audiences were largely FBI agents who investigated white-collar criminals but these were the prosecutors who pushed for convictions. Giving them the information they needed to bring criminals to justice would complete the circle.

But a game changer came when the conference organizers provided a list of questions I'd likely be asked.

The one that stopped me was this: "The Department of Justice receives Suspicious Activity Reports, referred to as SARs, sent to us by lenders whose loans have gone into foreclosure, and have reason to suspect fraud. Where can we look to figure out if wrong doing is going on in mortgage lending?"

At that moment, I flashed back to a recent conversation with my brother in which I worried out loud about the decline in my appraisal business. He shook his head.

"Don," he said, "You need to learn how to shut up."

I knew he had a point. All these presentations were filling a moral need for me, but they were also keeping clients aware that I'd been a whistleblower. If there was a choice between me and other appraisers – and there always was – I was more often than not losing out, and my savings were draining away.

When I saw the question about how to investigate Suspicious Activity Reports, I knew the answer would only deepen the financial hole I was digging for myself.

What federal prosecutors needed to know

The data these prosecutors needed to go after banks were already at their fingertips; they just didn't know it. They simply needed to turn to their colleagues at Freddie Mac and Fannie Mae and ask them nicely – like United States Attorneys can – for the information.

Here's why.

I knew that for the past three years or so, Freddie and Fannie had forced lenders to buy back $21 billion of home loans as part of a crackdown on faulty mortgages. So lenders had received tens of thousands of repurchase requests for loans they had insured. Freddie and Fannie had commissioned forensic reviews on the properties; these told the original appraisal value, the real value at the time of the loan, the amount of loss on each loan, who the appraisers and lenders were.

In other words, filed away at Freddie and Fannie offices were the paper trails the Department of Justice needed to find out if there was fraud, where it began, and who was responsible.

When I realized the Department of Justice didn't have this insight, I knew this revelation would be opening doors to more convictions. Disclosing this vital information would immediately bring to light lenders and appraisers who were cheating.

As expected, the question was raised, and I was ready with an answer. I had with me two appraisal reviews: one I had completed for the US Attorney's office in Kansas City, and the other for Fannie Mae for a repurchase demand due to a fraudulent appraisal. When the prosecutors studied them side-by-side, it wasn't hard to see how information from Fannie and Freddie could be used to prove fraud.

As I explained all this, I could hear people in the audience saying to each other, "So, it's civil..."

What was civil? What was this about?

As it turned out, the Department of Justice had been looking for a way to hold big banks accountable for what happened between 2005 and 2010. Up to now they'd considered bringing criminal cases against the banks and bankers responsible.

But criminal cases are difficult to prosecute, and success in getting a guilty verdict might be nearly impossible.

Not so if, instead of criminal charges, the government came after the banks with a civil suit, where standards of proof aren't as stringent.

Of course, that's exactly what happened, and on September 2, 2011 the Department of Justice sued 17 banks – including Bank of America and JPMorgan Chase & Co. - and 21 individuals for a total of $196 billion dollars. When the cases were settled, these defendants paid out more than $62 billion in fines.

For the integrity of the system, wonderful!

For me, I knew the disclosure of this information would likely mean the end of my appraisal career. These mortgage lenders were my clients. To be providing law enforcement simple ways to hold them accountable would mean business finally drying up completely.

I left South Carolina understanding that hopes of a turn-around in my appraisal business were dead.

But another conversation kept me steady.

During lunch after my presentation, I wound up sharing stories with an assistant US attorney who prosecuted Mexican drug lords.

"This business we're involved in," she told me, "isn't for cowards. Because of the case I was prosecuting, the drug cartel put a bounty on my head. And the US Marshall's Service has driven my kids back and forth to school for the last year. We've had agents watching our house 24/7 for the same period."

Yet she hadn't quit.

How could I do less?

CHAPTER EIGHT

THE IMPACT

I wanted tougher penalties to push lenders into ethical behavior. And on July 21, 2010, the Dodd-Frank Wall Street Reform and Consumer Protection Act was signed into law.

Federal regulations with teeth

As I read through the new law's section on appraisal regulations, I found that four of the five recommendations I'd made at the Department of Justice Fraud Conference in 2009 were part of the law, and in 2016, the fifth was implemented via a regulatory change. Remember the five I'd pushed for in all those presentations?

1. Appraiser independence, with stiff fines for those who violate this rule.
2. Payment of Reasonable and Customary Fees to Appraisers.

3. Regulations of Appraisal Management Companies.

4. A Wall of Separation Between Appraisers and Lenders.

5. A 33% Rule, meaning that if a bank had its own Appraisal Management Company, only 1/3 of the appraisals they used could be generated by that AMC.

This bill marked a big victory, in my view. Back in 2008, the Missouri legislature had passed a similar bill, SB 1059, making it a felony to commit fraud.

SB 1059 "creates civil and criminal penalties for mortgage fraud and imposes sanctions upon certain licensed professionals and unlicensed individuals who commit the crime." The law's summary made clear exactly who it intended to target: real estate brokers and sales persons, residential mortgage brokers, and real estate appraisers.

Now Dodd-Frank could be used to enforce honesty on the national level.

Changing a huge and costly oversight

After the way we'd all suffered in the mortgage meltdown of 2008, I wasn't surprised by the passage of Dodd-Frank. What surprised me, perhaps, was how long it took to correct an enormously dangerous oversight in our legal system.

We live in a country where the rule of law results in thousands of laws on the books to regulate public, and sometimes private, life. For example, in the Missouri State Constitution even the occupation of barber is fully defined and his duty to honesty, integrity and legitimacy is detailed.

Our laws are so specific that in some states it is even illegal to feign blindness with the intension of robbing another person.

But in 2008 only eighteen states had laws declaring mortgage fraud a felony. No regulators were monitoring non-bank lenders for predatory lending practices. And the government hadn't prioritized investigations of mortgage fraud because they saw it as a "victimless crime."

Now that had changed. And I'd had the privilege of being part of driving the change.

I was also encouraged to see measures of change surface that I didn't expect. In 2010 Amy Heinz from Fannie Mae emailed me with a question.

She said her office had noticed that a recent report from the Financial Crimes' Enforcement Network listed Missouri as the top state for 2009 Suspicious

Activity Reports (SARs) in the nation – both in volume and percentage. Missouri even beat California and Florida. In 2007 there were only 1,481 mortgage fraud SARs filed in Missouri, but by 2009 the number is 11,895! And this number represented a full 18% of the SARs submitted in the nation. That's nearly one in five reports of potential fraud – and coming from just one state.

"Any idea what contributed to this huge presence?" she asked.

It wasn't that we were so much more dishonest in Missouri, I told her. Maybe along with the massive publicity resulting from our trial back in 2007, presentations by people like FBI Agent Julia Jensen and myself had made people better equipped to spot fraud, and to know who to call when they saw it.

Mortgage lending and securities: celebrating what changed

A number of things have changed for the better since the meltdown largely due to new regulations at the federal and state level. Here is at least a partial list of changes:

1. Severed Connections:
Previously, appraisers had relationships with lenders

directly. Now, lenders cannot have direct access to appraisers; they must go through a third party (Appraisal Management Companies).

2. Strengthened Insurance Reviews: Previously, Fannie Mae and Freddie Mac did not review files before they insured loans. Now, all data and appraisals are reviewed before insuring loans.

3. Appraiser Independence: Previously, appraisers could be told by lenders what value they were seeking before they would order an appraisal, and lenders wouldn't pay for an appraisal that lacked the value they wanted. Now, appraiser independence is mandated in Dodd-Frank to separate the origination and valuation of properties.

4. Adjusted Down Payments: Previously, lenders developed lending programs that encouraged realtors to add 6% to the listing price to cover the down payment. Now, the seller can only pay up to 3% of the cost. Buyers have to come with at least 3% down.

5. Comprehensive Appraisal Reviews: Previously, 5-10% of appraisals were reviewed for quality control. Now, 100% of appraisals are reviewed prior to funding.

6.   Reduced Inflated Values: Previously, 44% of appraisals (between 2004-2009} were intentionally inflated on their values. Now, only 4% of appraisals have shown misevaluation.

7.   Enhanced Loan Underwriting: Previously nine million properties were foreclosed on between 2008-2011. On loans made since 2012, only 1% have gone into default.

8.   Independent Appraisal Management Companies (AMCs): Previously, lenders utilized AMCs they owned so lenders could charge borrowers $600 for the appraisal and pay appraisers only $200. Now, lenders cannot own AMCs. Plus, ten states have passed laws that define what a "reasonable and customary fee" will be, and AMCs must pay that fee.

9.   Expanded Criminal Laws: Previously, it was a felony in only 17 states to commit mortgage fraud. Now, it is against state and federal law to commit mortgage fraud.

10.   More Reporting Opportunities: Previously, there were no hotlines to report mortgage or appraisal fraud. Now, HUD, the FBI, the Consumer Protection Bureau and states have ways to report fraud.

11.   Securities: Previously, investment banks packaged together loans and sold them as mortgage-backed securities. Now, private label ending is 10% of what it was before 2008. Fannie Mae and Freddie Mac were put in conservatorship by the government.

12.   Securities Content: Previously, to get higher returns, mortgage-backed securities contained A-credit, B-credit, Alt-A and subprime loans. Now, mortgage-backed securities are mostly A-borrowers with lower loan-to-value ratios.

13.   Verified Properties: Previously, loans were made on houses that did not exist. Now, all homes are verified by USPS address.

14.   "Blind Appraisals": Previously, lenders wrote in the value they required on the appraisal order form. Now, no value or required loan amount can be written on the order form.

15.   Capped Loan Fees: Previously, lenders charged borrowers up to 10% of the loan as fees. Now, lenders' maximum profit on a loan is capped at 3% of the loan.

16.   Disbursed Loan Control: Previously, the top five lenders/banks controlled 67% of home loans. Now, the top five lenders control 45% of home loans.

17.   Verification of Funds: Previously, there was no verification of funds to close on sales. Now, borrowers must show proof of funds sixty days prior to closing.

18.   Loan Packaging Reviews: Previously, when loans were packaged together 5-10% were sent for review appraisals. Now, lenders must review 10% post-closing and all prior for inaccurate information.

19.   Automated Review Response: Previously, if the review appraisal showed a lower amount than the first appraisal, banks would include the loan in a different package of loans for sale. Now, loans and appraisals are sent through underwriting electronically to verify the information is correct.

20.   Process-wide Oversight: Previously, there was no regulation of the parties involved in real estate transactions. Now, license numbers tracks appraisals and lenders and loan officers have ID numbers to track them. Title companies and AMCs are licensed in 39 states. Loans are reviewed by six people in the process of approval. Appraisers are removed from approved lists for faculty appraisals.

Just one person...

I didn't set out to help change the law. In fact, if you'd told me that was ahead, I'd have laughed. Soccer dad from Leawood, Kansas? Fairly boring real estate appraiser?

Looking back, all this started with a long string of small choices. I'd find a fellow appraiser who performed a series of dishonest appraisals, and ask our licensing board to investigate. These were not heroic acts, just a guy doing the best he could to help a profession he cared about stay honest.

In time, a moment came when one of these small decisions drove a phone call that changed my life, and helped change the laws of our nation.

Of course much of what followed was the confluence of forces well beyond my control. FBI Special Agent Julia Jensen, who led the work on our case, calls this "What were the odds?"

She recounts, in this case, what were the odds:
- The bad guys would call an honest appraiser?
- That appraiser would know who to call?
- The honest appraiser would be willing to cooperate with the FBI?
- The government would be able to identify the lender?

- That lender would cooperate?
- The bad guys would incriminate themselves?

All together, these factors created a perfect storm of real-time evidence to break up a fraud ring pulling off seventeen million dollars in illegal activity. And I could never have created this perfect storm. But I could be part of this larger impact because dozens of times before I'd chosen to do right when it would have been easier to ignore the wrong.

Life changes not in one huge act, but in a thousand little acts that together make a difference.

And an epilogue...

Rousing success would make a great finish to a story like this. The hero wins the gold medal and gets the girl. But for me, there was no gold medal.

At the same time the industry regulations I'd worked for were beginning to be enforced, I finally admitted there wouldn't be a way any longer to save the business. In 2012, I declared bankruptcy.

We closed up shop, and along with the business, I lost real estate investments meant to fund my kids' college educations. I moved from my house to an apartment, leaving behind a solid credit rating and a bucketful of memories.

But the biggest hit, I think, was to my pride. I'm from a family of die-hard independents who were sure in our ability to make our own way, and not owe anybody anything. We kept our noses clean, gave a day's work for a day's wage, and always, always paid our bills.

Plus, I'd been appraising successfully for nearly thirty years in a business initially started with my dad so, besides a lifetime of work, family pride was part of the mix in a way I couldn't explain well, but knew was true.

Friends tried to console me with stories of other real estate related business owners who had lost out, but it didn't help. I'd always covered my bases, prepared by saving for the rainy times by stowing away cash during the good times. But this time I couldn't wait any longer. The pressure of clients lost to my FBI connections proved to be the tipping point.

After the fall

In the years since, I have come back professionally, hired as Chief Appraiser by Pendo, a newly forming independent appraisal management company that wanted to build its reputation on quality, ethical work. We were an obvious fit, and in the years since have grown considerably. At the end of our first year in business in 2013, we had grossed

$8.5 million; by 2016 we had nearly tripled that amount. We've been honored with the "fastest growing business in Kansas City" designation, and made the list of *Inc.* magazine's "Fastest-growing 500."

Besides finding success again in my professional life, my kids have completed college and launched successful careers, and I'm now a homeowner again.

But more importantly, after the roller coaster ride that came from telling the truth to the FBI and others, a new definition of failure and success came to me.

Whether or not you fail depends on what reward you're after

In 2011 my son Daniel asked me to read an essay he'd written for a college class in Ethics. "I want you to read it," he said, "because I got a great grade on it – and because it's about you."

He told the story of what we came to call the $800,000 phone call and my subsequent work with the FBI, then educating other influencers about how to stop mortgage fraud.

Then he said this:

"One man in the right place is given two options: to do what is just and make life better for more than just himself, or do what is unjust, the more profitable choice. Should he let fraud go on, as others were doing, and justify the money as a way to support two teenagers as a single parent?"

"He listened to the words he had been teaching me as I grew up, and chose the right action, though this choice left his name tainted and cost his business. The sacrifices my dad made left him with more stress at home and less money than before."

"But I would not respect him as much as I do now if he had not made the choices he did."

When I read Daniel's words, five years of struggle were suddenly worth any price they exacted. What looked like failure had generated my greatest success. I wanted to leave my children a legacy of honesty and a will to choose the right when the choice presents itself.

That happened.

It's enough.

DONALD J. GOSSMAN

Donald J. Gossman, SRA is considered a leading authority on appraisal fraud, and has over 37 years of experience in the industry.

He holds the prestigious SRA designation from the Appraisal Institute and is a certified appraiser in seven states.

During his career he has served as President of the Kansas City Chapter of the Appraisal Institute, a member of the Missouri Appraiser Council, member of the Missouri Housing, Alliance, on the board of directors for the Kansas City Mortgage Bankers

Association and the Education Chairman of the Kansas City Appraisal Institute.

Mr. Gossman continues to work as a consultant on appraisal fraud and has been asked to speak as an expert by the US Attorney's office, Fannie Mae, the FBI and the Department of Justice. He has taught classes throughout the US to lawyers, bankers, realtors and licensing law officials.

He is currently Chief Appraiser for Pendo, which was named one of the faster growing companies in the US for the last 4 years by *Inc.* and *Ingram's* magazines.

He is father to a 25-year-old daughter who is a civil engineer and a 26-year-old son who holds a BSN in nursing.

* * * * * * * * * * * *

You can contact Don Gossman via email dgossman@pendomanagement.com or by visiting his website at dongossman.com for additional information and resources.